discovermore

Forms of Energy

What Is Heat Energy?

Virginia Elliott

Britannica Educational Publishing

IN ASSOCIATION WITH

THE ROSEN PUBLISHING GROUP

Published in 2026 by Britannica Educational Publishing (a trademark of Encyclopædia Britannica, Inc.) in association with The Rosen Publishing Group, Inc.
2544 Clinton Street, Buffalo, NY 14224

Distributed exclusively by Rosen Publishing.
To see additional Britannica Educational Publishing titles, go to rosenpublishing.com.

Editor: Danielle Haynes
Book Design: Michael Flynn

Photo Credits: Cover Mr.Somkeat/Shutterstock.com; (series background) Dai Yim/Shutterstock.com; p. 4 Lopolo/Shutterstock.com; p. 5 Cassiohabib/Shutterstock.com; p. 6 Olga_Shestakova/Shutterstock.com; p. 7 Peter Elvidge/Shutterstock.com; p. 8 PeopleImages.com - Yuri A/Shutterstock.com; p. 9 fuyu liu/Shutterstock.com; p. 10 nikkytok/Shutterstock.com; p. 11 OSweetNature/Shutterstock.com; p. 13 (top) Designua/Shutterstock.com; p. 13 (bottom) Dr. Me/Shutterstock.com; p. 14 Nandalal Sarkar/Shutterstock.com; p. 15 SeventyFour/Shutterstock.com; p. 16 KajaNi/Shutterstock.com; p. 17 siam.pukkato/Shutterstock.com; p. 19 (top) hanohiki/Shutterstock.com; pp. 19 (bottom), 23 Designua/Shutterstock.com; p. 20 DenisProduction.com/Shutterstock.com; p. 21 ADragan/Shutterstock.com; p. 22 Am.uhrinova/Shutterstock.com; p. 23 Designua/Shutterstock.com; p. 24 Bob1971/Shutterstock.com; p. 25 Johann Ragnarsson/Shutterstock.com; p. 26 isaputra/Shutterstock.com; p. 27 Ody_Stocker/Shutterstock.com; p. 28 Nicole Glass Photography/Shutterstock.com; p. 29 brgfx/Shutterstock.com.

Cataloging-in-Publication Data

Names: Elliott, Virginia (Children's writer).
Title: Heat energy / Virginia Elliott.
Description: New York : Britannica Educational Publishing, in association with Rosen Educational Services, 2026. | Series: Discover more: forms of energy | Includes glossary and index.
Identifiers: ISBN 9781641905664 (library bound) | ISBN 9781641905657 (pbk) | ISBN 9781641905671 (ebook)
Subjects: LCSH: Heat--Juvenile literature. | Thermodynamics--Juvenile literature.
Classification: LCC QC256.E45 2026 | DDC 536--dc23

Manufactured in China

CPSIA Compliance Information: Batch #QWBRIT26. For further information contact Rosen Publishing at 1-800-237-9932.

Contents

Get Moving

Playing hockey takes a lot of energy. You need energy to skate and hit the puck. All that activity may make you feel hot. Heat itself is a form of energy!

Energy is another word for power. It makes things move, machines work, and living things grow. There are many forms of energy, including chemical energy, sound energy, electrical energy, light energy, and heat energy. Heat energy is also called thermal energy. Each of these forms of energy can do work.

Exercising and playing sports can make you sweat and feel hot even when it's cold outside.

A roller coaster stopped at the top of a hill has potential energy, while a roller coaster going down a hill has kinetic energy.

All forms of energy can be described as either potential energy or kinetic energy. Potential energy is stored energy. An object with potential energy has the ability, or potential, to move. Kinetic energy is the energy of moving things. All moving objects, including a hockey player, have kinetic energy.

Consider This

Which of the forms of energy named on page four can be described as potential energy? Which can be described as kinetic energy?

The different types of energy can change from one form into another. With the use of a battery, stored chemical energy can change into electric energy. In a lightbulb, electric energy changes to light and heat. In fact, heat is often produced when energy changes forms.

One way heat is produced is through friction. Friction is a force that acts between two objects that are in contact with one another. It slows or stops movement between the two surfaces that are touching. The two objects require more moving energy, called **mechanical energy**, to work against the friction force.

Batteries store chemical energy, which is also considered potential energy until it's used.

Sometimes heat from friction can be so hot it hurts!

As the moving mechanical energy works against the friction, it transforms into heat energy. For example, you may have noticed that when you slide down or pull on a rope, your hands may feel hot as they rub against the rope.

WORD WISE

MECHANICAL ENERGY IS ALL THE ENERGY AN ENTIRE OBJECT HAS BECAUSE OF ITS MOTION AND ITS POSITION—OR ITS POTENTIAL ENERGY PLUS ITS KINETIC ENERGY.

Where Does Energy Come From?

The sun plays an important role in the generation of energy. It is the source of almost all energy on Earth. Heat and light from the sun help plants grow. In sunny areas, people use special devices to collect the heat of the sun and store it. That energy can be used to heat water and to heat houses. Other types of devices convert the sun's rays directly into electricity. This source of energy is known as solar energy.

Greenhouses can trap the heat from the sun to help plants grow even when it's cold outside.

Solar panels capture light energy from the sun and transform it into electrical energy.

In addition to the sun, both wind and water are used as sources of energy. For example, sailboats harness the power of the wind to move them along. Water mills use water flowing through rivers to turn wheels that grind grain or saw wood. Hydroelectric power plants use waterpower to produce electricity.

When we use wind or water to do work, we call them wind power and waterpower. Energy sources that are always available, such as the wind and water, are called **renewable** energy. Fossil fuels such as coal and oil, however, are limited.

WORD WISE

SOMETHING THAT IS RENEWABLE CAN BE REPLACED BY NATURE.

In Motion

Each object and being on Earth is made of particles called molecules. Molecules are always in motion. As an object is heated, the molecules in the object move faster. When this happens, the **temperature** of the object rises.

The temperature of a cup of hot chocolate is greater than the temperature of a cup of cold chocolate milk. The molecules in the hot chocolate are moving around more quickly than those in the cold chocolate milk. If the two cups are placed next to one another, heat will flow from the hot drink to the cold one. This is because heat always flows from hot objects to cool objects. The cool object absorbs the energy and becomes warmer.

When the molecules in water are boiled and move enough, they turn into their gaseous state and become steam.

When molecules are colder, as seen at the left of this image, they don't move as much.

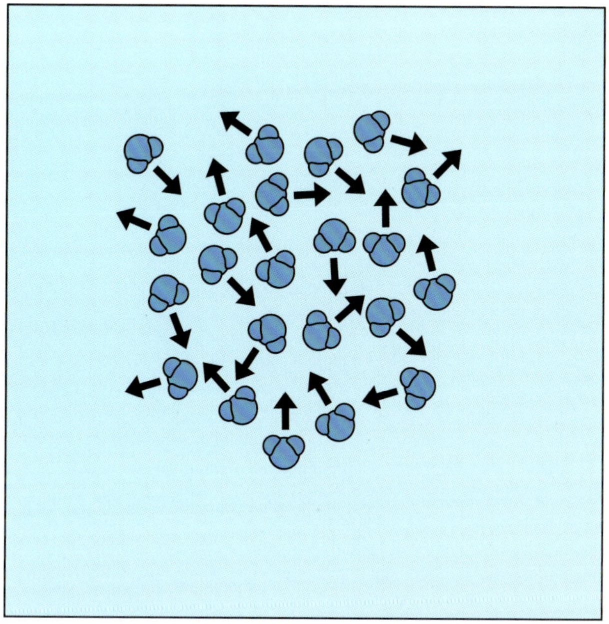

Slow Movement = Low Temperature
Contracted and Dense

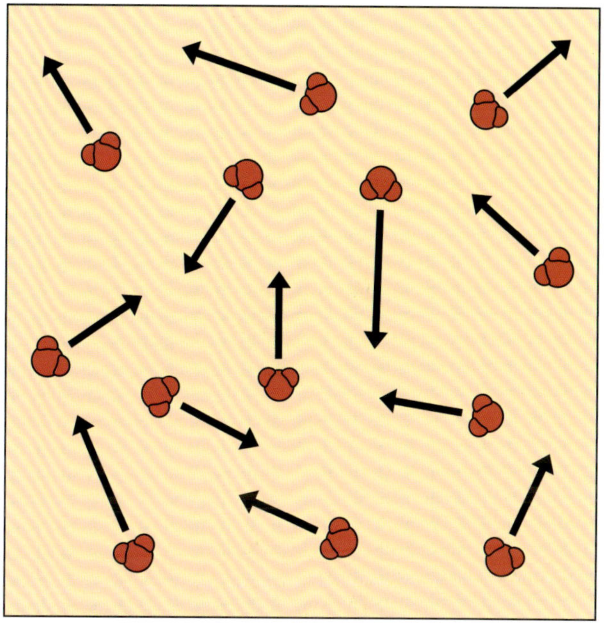

Fast Movement = High Temperature
Expanded and Less Dense

Heat energy is the total moving energy (or kinetic energy) of all the molecules in an object. All objects have heat energy, since the molecules that make up all objects are always moving. Even items that are cold to the touch or don't appear to be moving, such as ice, have heat energy.

WORD WISE

TEMPERATURE IS A MEASURE OF HOW HOT OR COLD SOMETHING IS.

Three States of Matter

All things in our world that take up space are called matter. Matter exists in different forms, called states. The three common states are solid, liquid, and gas.

Matter can change from one state to another when it is cooled or heated to a particular point. The temperature at which a liquid boils and turns into a gas is called its boiling point. That same temperature is called the condensation point when the gas condenses, or changes back into a liquid.

If cooled enough, the liquid will freeze and become a solid. The temperature at which a liquid becomes a solid is called its freezing point. For example, liquid water turns to ice when it is cooled to 32 °F (0 °C). The melting point for ice is the same temperature. Different types of matter have different boiling, melting, and freezing points. Most metals have very high melting points, but mercury is a liquid even at room temperature.

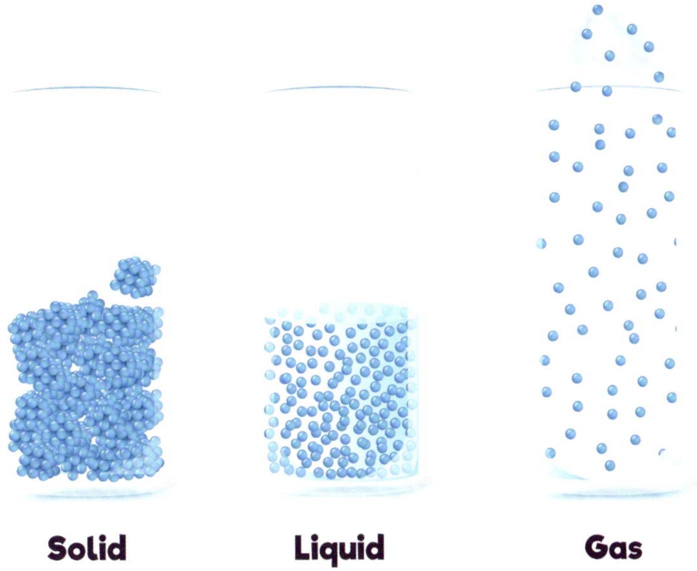

The temperature and how fast particles are moving determine whether something is a solid (such as ice), liquid (water), or gas (steam).

compareandcontrast

How are the states of a particular substance, such as water, similar? How are they different?

Mercury has a much lower freezing point than any other metal, -37.9 °F (-38.8 °C), a temperature not regularly found on Earth.

Heat energy moves from one object to another because of a difference in temperature between the two bodies. Most things in our world try to stay balanced, or even. This is true of heat energy, too. Heat always flows from warmer objects to cooler objects. As heat is **transferred** from the warmer object, the temperature of that object decreases. As the cool object absorbs the heat, its temperature rises.

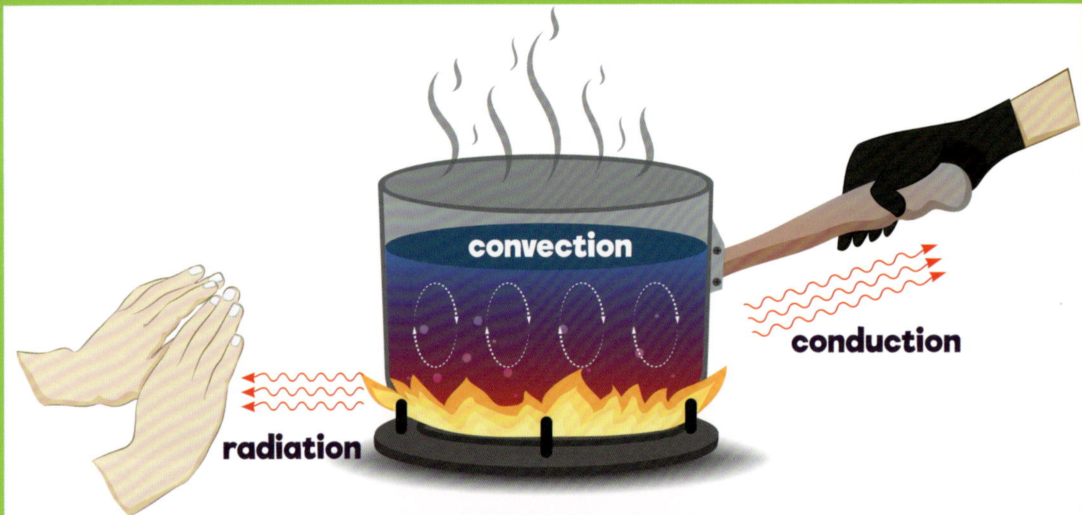

Heat transfers, or travels, to cooler objects by either conduction, convection, or radiation.

If you touch a shirt right after you've ironed it, it'll be hot!

Heat travels in three ways: by conduction, by convection, and by radiation. Conduction is the flow of heat inside an object. It is also the flow of heat between objects in contact with each other. Conduction occurs in solids, liquids, or gases that are at rest. Energy flows, but the substance through which the heat is being transferred does not itself flow. An example is the flow of heat from a hot iron to the clothes we're ironing.

WORD WISE

WHEN SOMETHING IS TRANSFERRED, IT MOVES FROM ONE PLACE TO ANOTHER.

Convection

Convection is the movement of heat transported by a liquid or gas. An example is heating water in a teakettle. As water is heated, the water molecules rise and the heat spreads.

Natural convection occurs when fluids—that is, liquids and gases—are heated. When a fluid is heated, it becomes less dense or compact. The molecules speed up and spread out. A warmer volume of fluid will rise, while a colder and thus more compacted volume of fluid will sink.

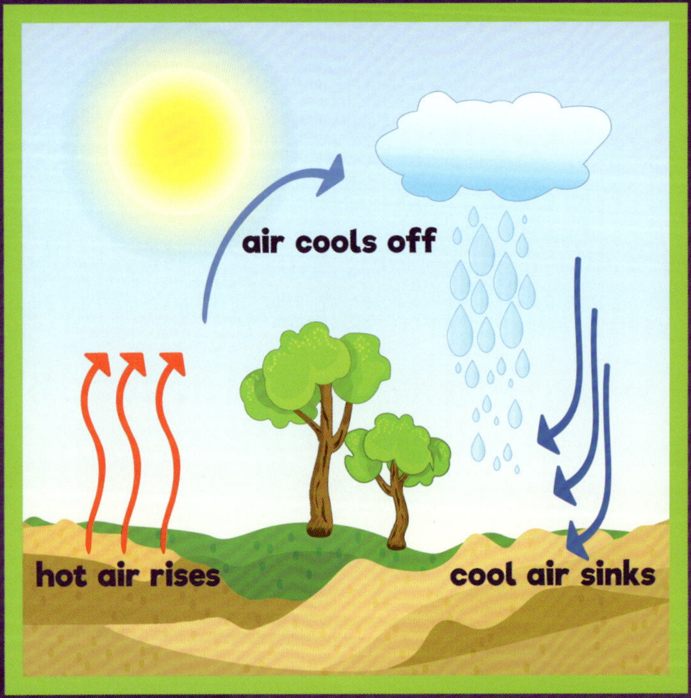

Both indoors and outdoors, hot air rises while cool air sinks. That's because hot air is less dense and rises above more compact cold air.

The energy that causes a hot-air balloon to rise is an example of convection. The heated air inside the balloon wants to rise above the cooler air outside of it.

Other convection currents can occur in the atmosphere, the layer of gas that surrounds Earth. These convection currents move vertically (up and down) and cause winds and thunderstorms.

Forced convection is when fluids or gases are moved by outside forces, not by a change in temperature. This happens in convection ovens, where a fan inside the oven moves heat from the heating element.

Consider This

How might the sun affect the currents in the atmosphere and therefore the weather?

Radiation

The third and final way heat is moved is through radiation. Heat radiation is the flow of heat between objects that are not in contact with each other. For example, someone standing near a hot stove or fire will feel the heat from the stove.

Another example of radiation is the heat that radiates from the sun. Radiation from the sun gives Earth most of its heat. Energy from the sun also helps plants, such as trees, grow. Eventually the wood from a tree can be burned to provide more heat.

Radiation from the sun travels in all directions through space and some kinds of matter. Finally, the radiation strikes a body, such as a planet, where it is absorbed. The heat energy of the body increases, and its temperature rises. This type of heat energy is also known as thermal radiation.

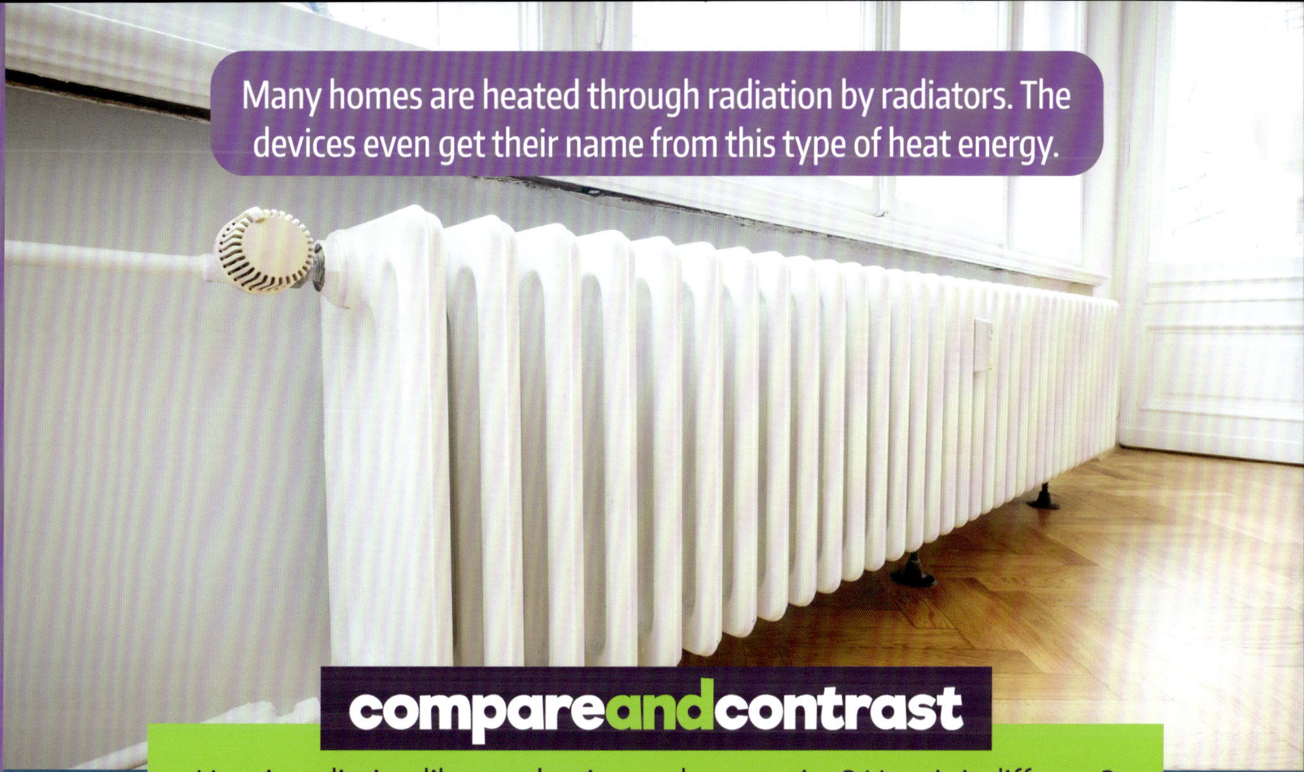

Many homes are heated through radiation by radiators. The devices even get their name from this type of heat energy.

compare and contrast

How is radiation like conduction and convection? How is it different?

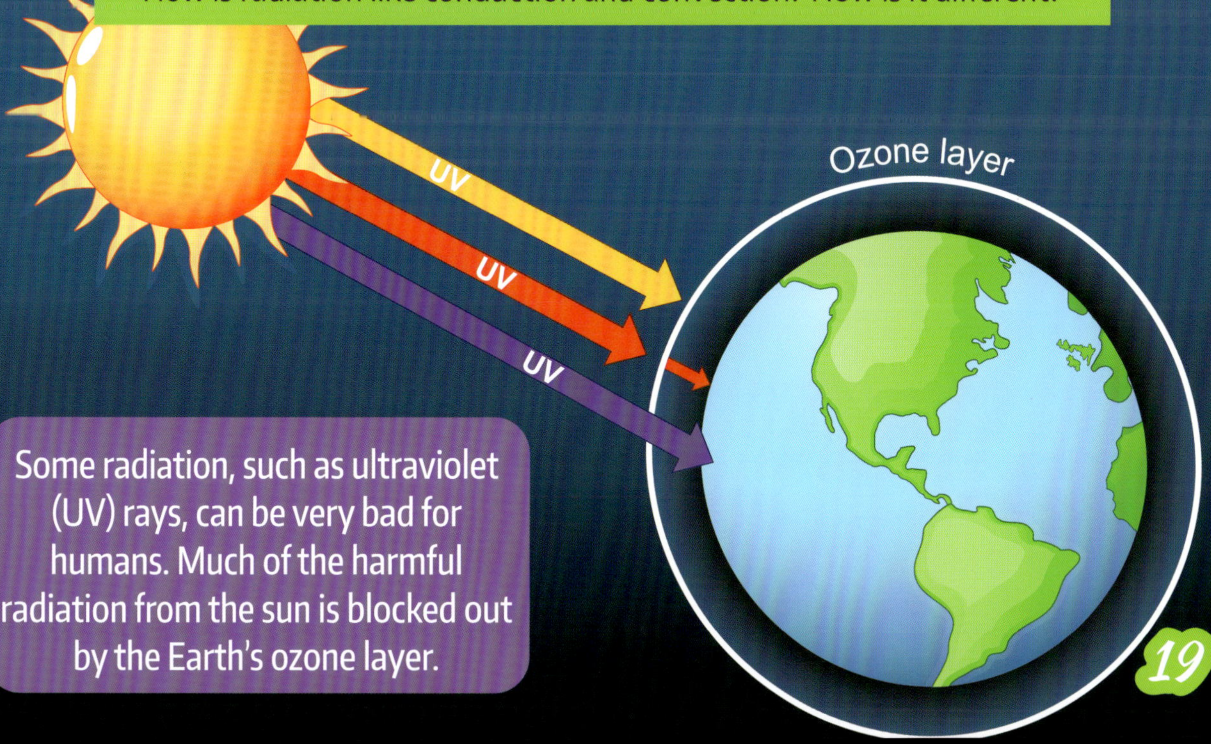

Some radiation, such as ultraviolet (UV) rays, can be very bad for humans. Much of the harmful radiation from the sun is blocked out by the Earth's ozone layer.

Taking the Temperature

How do we know how hot or cold things are? Heat is so well known from our earliest childhood that we hardly think about it. A steaming bowl of soup feels hot, while a book sitting on a table in your room does not. An ice cube feels cold.

Each of those feelings is really a measure of the heat energy in each object. This is because temperature is a measure of how fast, on average, the molecules in something are moving.

We know not to touch fire because it will be too hot. But how can we find out how hot it is?

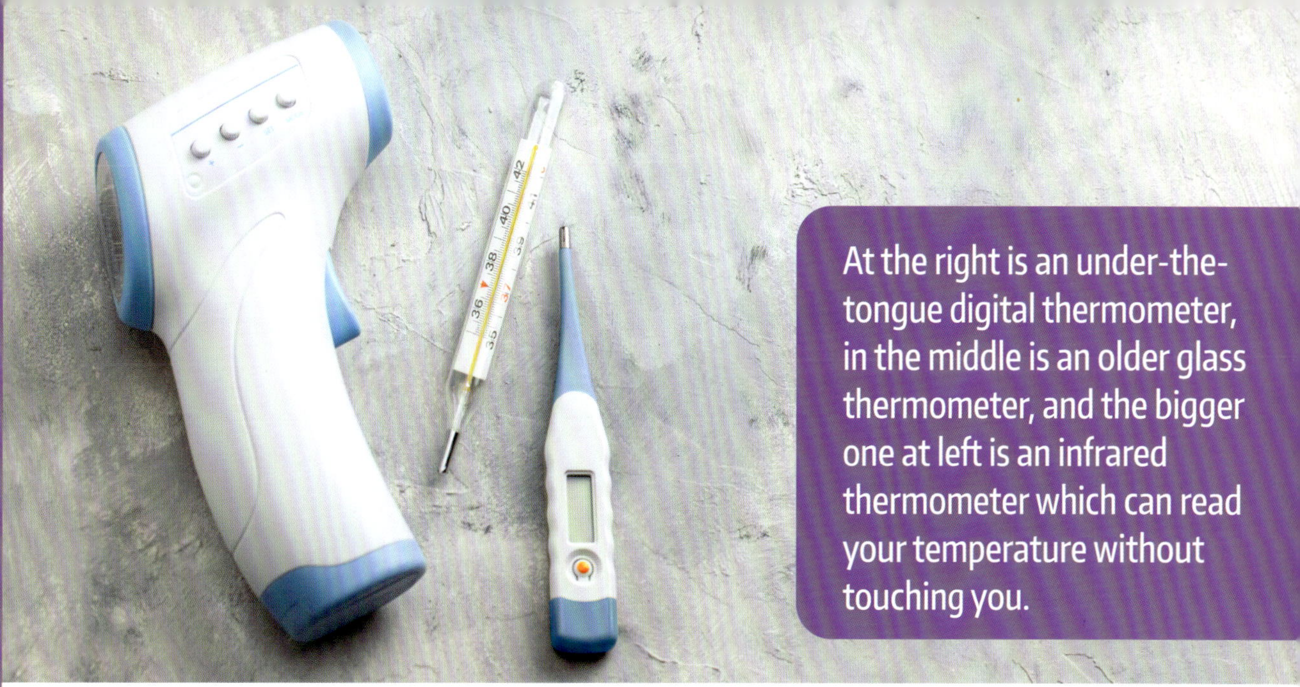

At the right is an under-the-tongue digital thermometer, in the middle is an older glass thermometer, and the bigger one at left is an infrared thermometer which can read your temperature without touching you.

Heating a bowl of soup, for example, raises the temperature of the soup by speeding up the average motion of the soup's molecules.

We use thermometers to measure temperature. A basic thermometer is a small glass tube with some liquid inside. The liquid expands as its temperature is raised. Lines on the tube tell what the temperature is, based on how high the liquid rises as it expands. Today, most people use digital thermometers.

Consider This

Can you remember the last time you used or saw a thermometer?

Scales

Temperature, like any other measurement, is shown as a number on a scale. A scale is a series of spaces marked by lines that is used as a system for measuring something. On a thermometer, each space marked by lines is a unit known as a degree.

Three different temperature scales are in general use: Fahrenheit, Celsius, and Kelvin. In the United States, we use the Fahrenheit temperature scale daily when we check the weather before heading off to work or school. The Kelvin and Celsius temperature scales are widely used for scientific measurement. The Celsius temperature scale is also used in everyday life in most parts of the world. It is also known as the centigrade temperature scale.

Most outdoor thermometers show both the Celsius and Fahrenheit scales. Kelvin is mostly used by scientists.

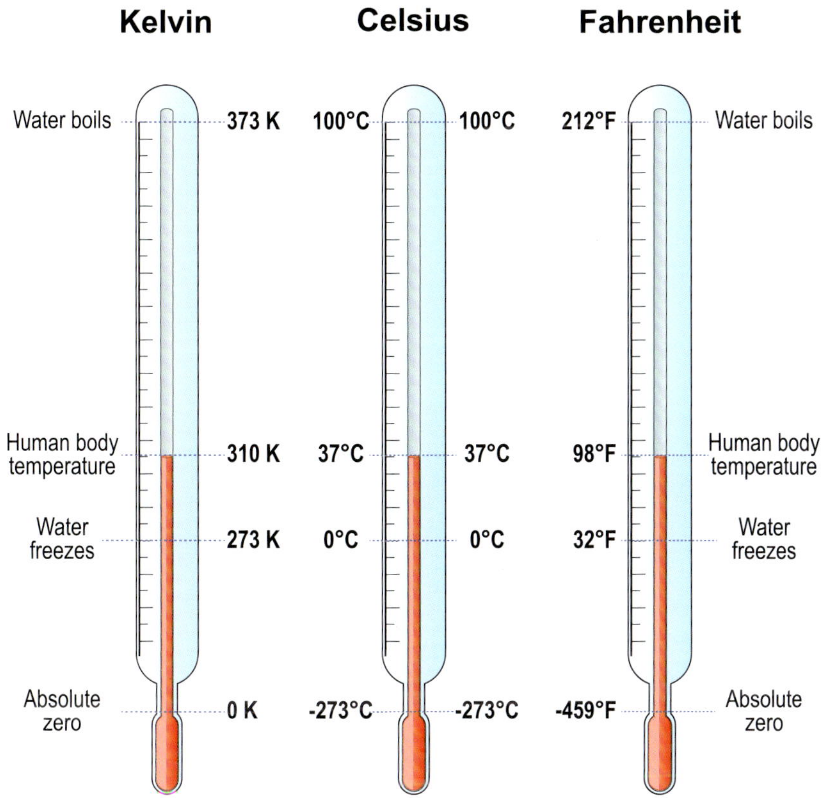

Here's a look at how the Kelvin, Celsius, and Fahrenheit scales compare to each other.

You can pick any of the scales to measure the temperature of something. For example, water freezes at 0° (zero degrees) on the Celsius scale, 32° on the Fahrenheit scale, and 273° on the Kelvin scale. A fourth scale, called the Rankine scale, is used only by certain kinds of engineers.

Consider This

Why do you think there is more than one temperature scale?

Putting Heat to Work

Heat is just like any other form of energy—it can do lots of work. When heat is added to a liquid, the molecules of the liquid move faster and farther apart. If enough heat is added to the liquid, the molecules may move so far from each other that the liquid will boil and change into a gas. The molecules in the gas can exert a great pushing force as they get hotter and spread farther apart. The pushing force exerted by heated gas molecules is often used to do work.

Early trains used steam to power them. The trains burned coal to create heat, which then heated water to create steam.

The small country of Iceland relies on geothermal energy more than any other nation in the world. That's because it has many volcanoes, which create lots of underground heat.

We use heat energy to cook, keep warm in winter, and power our machines. Many power plants produce heat energy by burning substances, such as coal, to boil water, creating steam. The steam rises and turns a series of blades. The turning blades provide power to a turbine, which produces electricity. Geothermal power plants use high-pressure hot water and steam from deep inside Earth to create power.

Consider This

Steam engines were once used to power trains, ships, and cars. What fuels do you think were burned to produce heat energy for the steam engine?

Heat and the Environment

Most power plants don't run on renewable resources like geothermal heat. Many plants burn fossil fuels, such as coal, to produce the heat energy they run on. Fossil fuels include petroleum, natural gas, and coal. These are used to run factories, heat homes, and power automobiles.

Petroleum, or oil, is drilled from inside Earth using platforms in the middle of the ocean. If there is an accident, the oil can spill into the ocean and harm wildlife.

Cars that run on gasoline emit gases that are harmful to the planet and your health.

Fossil fuels are the remains of things that lived long ago. When plants and animals die, they break down and decay. Over millions of years this process produces fossil fuels. The planet's supply of fossil fuels is limited. Fossil fuels are **nonrenewable** resources.

We must be responsible about how we get heat energy. The fossil fuels that we burn to make heat energy can harm our planet. When petroleum and coal burn, they release gases. These gases react with moisture to produce acid rain, a dangerous form of pollution. They can also harm the atmosphere.

WORD WISE

ONCE SOMETHING NONRENEWABLE IS USED UP, IT WILL BE GONE FOREVER.

Fossil fuels are harmful to the Earth's atmosphere, which traps thermal energy from the sun. This can lead to a problem called global warming. Carbon dioxide (CO_2) and other gases in the air do this trapping. They are called greenhouse gases. This process is called the greenhouse effect, after the greenhouses that keep seedlings warm and protected.

Without these gases too much heat would go back into space, and living things could not survive. However, scientists think that human activities are increasing the greenhouse effect. Burning fossil fuels release greenhouse gases into the air, and the extra gases trap more heat.

Human activities have led to climate change, which is the long-term shift in weather patterns and temperatures on Earth.

Greenhouse gases include carbon dioxide (CO_2), methane (CH_4), and nitrous oxide (N_2O).

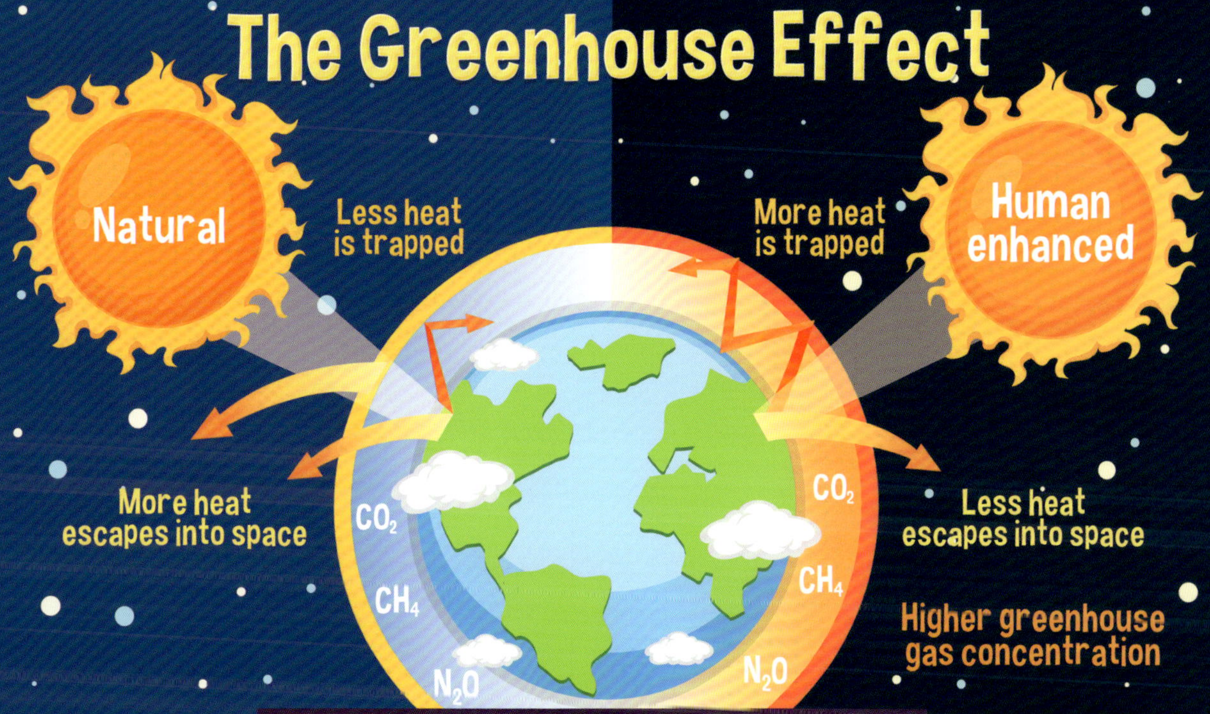

compare and contrast

In what ways are a plant greenhouse and our atmosphere alike, or different?

The average surface temperature on Earth is slowly increasing. This trend is known as global warming. Global warming is the reason polar ice is melting and sea levels are rising. Many scientists believe that we must find a solution to make our planet safe for the future. They suggest more people use renewable forms of energy, such as solar, wind, and geothermal.

Glossary

absorb To take in.
chemical Matter that can be mixed with other matter to cause changes.
condense To make dense or more compact.
contact When objects are in contact, their surfaces are touching.
convert To change from one substance, form, use, or unit to another.
decay To rot or break down.
dense Something that is compact.
expand To increase in size, number, or amount.
fuel A material used to produce heat or power by burning.
generate To create.
global Having to do with the whole world.
harness To use.
infrared Referring to rays of light that can't be seen and are longer than rays that produce red light.
mercury A silvery metal that is liquid at normal temperatures.
molecule The smallest unit of a substance that has all the properties of that substance.
natural gas Gas that comes from Earth's crust through natural openings or drilled wells.
particle One of the very small parts of matter (such as a molecule, atom, or electron).
petroleum An oily flammable liquid that is the source of gasoline, kerosene, fuel oils, and other products.
transform To change from one thing to another.
turbine An engine in which the pressure of a fluid (such as water, steam, or air) spins a series of blades.

For More Information

Books

Hardyman, Robyn. *Geothermal Energy*. Bridgnorth, UK: Cheriton Children's Books, 2022.

Kenney, Karen Latchana. *Energy from Natural Gas.* Minneapolis, MN: Bearport Publishing Company, 2022.

O'Daly, Anne. *Amazing Activities with Heat and Energy.* New York, NY: Enslow Publishing, 2023.

Websites

Britannica Kids: Heat

www.kids.britannica.com/kids/article/heat/390761

This website includes more information about heat energy, including photos and diagrams.

NASA: Climate Kids

www.climatekids.nasa.gov/kids-guide-to-climate-change

Read more about climate change and how it differs from weather.

Publisher's note to educators and parents: Our editors have carefully reviewed these websites to ensure that they are suitable for students. Many websites change frequently, however, and we cannot guarantee that a site's future contents will continue to meet our high standards of quality and educational value. Be advised that students should be closely supervised whenever they access the internet.

Index